ROMEO 1-1

Vietnam Tour of Duty

A Personal Diary

J a m e s   M c G i n n i s

PAGE PUBLISHING
Conneaut Lake, PA

First originally published by Page Publishing 2022

ISBN 978-1-6624-7978-6 (pbk)
ISBN 979-8-88654-435-0 (hc)
ISBN 978-1-6624-7979-3 (digital)

Printed in the United States of America

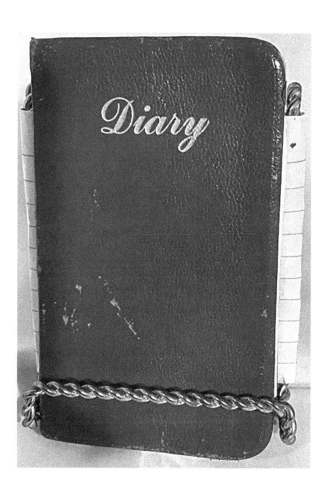

To Denny.

To my family and friends, and to all who
served during the Vietnam War.
Autumn 2021

Author's Ribbons and Medals Award

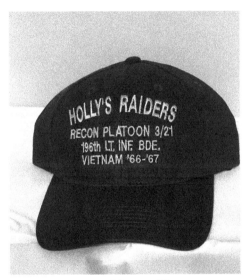

Recon Platoon Hat

Romeo 1-1

Vietnam—Tour of Duty

A Personal Diary

By James McGinnis

United States Army

October 7, 1965—July 13, 1967

196TH LIGHT INFANTRY BRIGADE

Delta Company 3rd Battalion 21st Infantry Regiment

Recon Platoon (Holly's Raiders)

Vietnam July 15, 1966—July 12, 1967

Foreword

I look back fondly on my time growing up in Union City, New Jersey in the fifties. We lived in the projects or in apartments, some in cold water flats with shared bathrooms in the hallways, some lucky enough to have a modest home. We weren't in poverty, but families often eked by paycheck to paycheck. The corner grocery store kept a running tab so people could buy food and pay when they had the money. We made friends easily and kept them for life. We went to school together, played sports together, and sometimes shared baseball gloves and football helmets so no one was left out. We watched out for one another, and we bonded. We shared the same good values taught by our parents including respect and love of country.

Jim McGinnis was my closest friend, as was George, Tony, Jimmy, and Jackie. Even after we graduated high school, we hung out every day, played ball, double-dated, sang Kingston Trio and Clancy Brothers songs, and as the draft was still in existence, we all received our "greetings" around the same time. Although at the time, I didn't think so, I was lucky to be designated 1Y. But all my friends were 1A and were preparing to leave home in a few weeks, some in the army, some in the marines, to possibly go to a war zone to fight in a country most people couldn't point to on a map.

I was always interested in history and read many Civil War diaries that gave firsthand accounts of their experiences. This gave us insight as to what a soldier went through daily: camp life, their equipment, the food they ate, the weather, the local terrain, and of course, skirmishes and battles.

Knowing that Jim had a sharp wit and an ability to notice or recognize things, I gave him a diary and told him that he should keep a daily journal of his experiences for future generations. This is the result. When you read this diary, you are with him on the boat, heading to Nam and throughout his tour of duty up until his return to the States. You are there with him every step of the way. He is very detailed, giving you names of other soldiers, officers, weather, patrols, etc. Once you start reading you will not put it down until you finish it. You may see some words you are not familiar with like *blantz*. That was a term we used growing up to describe what in World War II jargon would be fubar. You will soon figure it out.

This diary is also important in that Viet Nam was the last war that will have a personal written record with letters and diaries. Since then, everything is electronic. You can print emails, but it's not the same as reading handwritten accounts as they are occurring in real time.

Thankfully, God protected my friends and all the lower Union City boys returned home safely, and to this day we still call each other every day and go to lunch or dinner regularly. However, I still remember the day that I drove up to the Selective Service Center to say goodbye to Jim and Tony as they boarded the bus to take them to Fort Dix, and as the bus pulled away, the words of one of our favorite Clancy Brothers songs, "The Parting Glass," ran through my head.

Of all the comrades that e'er I had
They're sorry for my going away
And all the sweethearts that e'er I had
They'd wish me one more day to stay
But since it falls unto my lot
That I should rise, and you should not
I gently rise and softly call
Good night and joy be with you all

Dennis Buttacavoli
Hasbrouck Heights, New Jersey

Preface

The diary I had with me throughout my tour of duty in Vietnam from July 1966 until July 1967 was given to me by my friend Dennis, I call him Denny. Many times, when I was writing in the diary, I had in mind that I was writing to Denny. That friend and his mother picked me up at Fort Dix, New Jersey. When I arrived home from my tour of duty, all these years, I've kept my diary close to me, and it has been an important part of my life. If you ask me how my day is going now, I can look back to the same day during my year in Vietnam. It gives me an instant perspective.

I hope this diary will give you some perspective, too, and insight from inside my tour of duty. It is not entirely easy to share this as it has been over fifty-four years since I wrote it, and Denny saw it for the first time a few months ago. I think I needed to be ready to share it. My time as a tour guide at the New Jersey Vietnam Veterans' Memorial, Museum, and Educational Center has helped me. If you suffer from PTSD, as I do, I hope you will find the kind of support I have had, and I encourage you to reach out for help. The VA is there for you as everyone needs help sometimes.

For each day, I wrote only a few lines for this book; I've annotated some of the entries to give you additional information. My close colleague in this endeavor is Nora Thompson, I call her my niece. We first met when she took a tour of the New Jersey Vietnam Veterans' Memorial, Museum, and Educational Center in 2019. It was Nora's idea to have the diary published. She then typed the entire manuscript from my handwritten diary in the summer of 2021 before starting her junior year at Rutgers University. She provides encouragement and suggestions. She is my chosen editor.

The foreword is written by Denny; without him, the diary would never have been written.

A Special Thanks To

My Editor, Nora Thompson, and her family. For listening to my stories from my Vietnam War Diary and for instilling in me the compassion to bring to others an eyewitness account of my war experiences in great detail as I wrote them, not from memory but from, in most cases, the very same day or one or two days later. These passages were written by me, a combat veteran Recon Scout as I experienced or viewed them from a "place far away" and a "long time ago" and for the first time to share with others. This is truly a historic memoir from a soldier who answered his nation's call and served both honorably and faithfully when he was called to serve.

.

Note on Meanings
of Some Terms

Nora, editor, with Author

As Denny says in his foreword, some terms used in the diary, such as *blantz*, do not need explaining. You can get them from context. An example is *buku* in the diary, which means "a lot" (and sounds like "beaucoup" in French). In response to Nora's questions, I have explained a few things, and here are her questions and my answers:

NORA. What is the big red?
JIM: The 1st Infantry Division.

NORA: What was Lan's Laundry exactly?
JIM: Like a general store.

NORA: What is Goliath's?
JIM: Goliath's is Viet Laundry.

NORA: What or who is Sally?
JIM: Sally's is Filipino Bar.

NORA: What was R+R? What did it stand for?
JIM: Stands for Rest and Recreation.

NORA: What does PHILCAG mean?
JIM: Philippine Civic Action Group.

NORA: Can you remind me what *num qua* means?
JIM: Hassle.

NORA: Does PX stand for post exchange?
JIM: Yes.

NORA: Does PLT stand for platoon?
JIM: Yes.

NORA: What does LZ mean?
JIM: Landing Zones.

NORA: What does "in rubber" mean?
JIM: Means Rubber Trees Plantation.

NORA: What does A-O-BLUE mean?
JIM: Means Area of Operation A-Blue designation by the army.

NORA: What is "Mad Minute"?
JIM: Means everybody fires their weapons together for one minute.

NORA: What is "H+I"?
JIM: Means Harassment and Interdiction artillery barrage.

NORA: What does AFR stand for?
JIM: Means Armed Forces Radio Station.

NORA: In your May 13ᵗʰ entry, who is "Tom"?
JIM: Vietnamese Merchant.

NORA: What does IG mean?
JIM: IG means Inspector General.

NORA: What does MACV mean?
JIM: MACV means Military Assistance Command, Vietnam.

July

July 15

We left Boston Harbor at 2:00 p.m. The sleeping quarters are four high. I'm on the bottom. The food is good. Some are getting seasick. I'm holding out.

July 16

I have twelve hours KP in bakeshop every two days. Tony is on a different shift. Good movie other night: George Raft 1940. The ocean is beautiful out here. Had to lose one-hour time near Florida.

July 17

Lost one-hour time tonight. Might re-up in navy. Chow is better. Heat is unbearable in sleeping quarters. Wish I could sleep on deck. Sang "Sloop John B" tonight with the others.

July 18

Today we passed Cuba and Guantanamo Bay. A sight to behold. The Caribbean Sea is beautiful *plus colors* here. We saw sharks and porpoise follow the boat. Should hit Panama tomorrow.

July 19

We had boat drill today. What a blantz, we all would have gone down with the ship if it was real. No Panama today. Tropical sun is hot.

July 20

We entered canal at 6:30 a.m. Took pictures. Went through five locks. Jungle all over perpetual rain. Getting colder, should hit Bay of Mexico tomorrow.

July 21

We are in the open sea again. Passed Costa Rica today. Should hit Mexico tomorrow or next day. The weather is much cooler. Getting fat in the bakery.

July 22

Passed Guatemala today. Now are off coast of Southern California. Launched note in bottle. Saw picture on deck, "The Thrill of It All" was good.

July 23

We passed Acapulco today. Too bad we couldn't stop by. Played bingo tonight. I got close, but I didn't win anything. The trip is getting more boring.

July 24

About one thousand miles from Long Beach. Should get there on the 26th. Gumba and I took pictures with my "swinger." He is sending your picture with a letter.

July 25

Another day on the dreary sloop John Patch. Saw a movie tonight: The Courtship of Eddie's Father. The warm California sun isn't so warm. Temperature: sixty-five degrees.

July 26

Main highlight we got into Long Beach tonight. Tied one on and *blew my cool* at Navy PX. Met navy medic from Jersey City. Sweet dreams.

July 27

Went back to base at 3:30. Took pictures and called home. Carrier *Yorktown* came home from

Virginia today. Big reception. Saw night softball game. Sorry I didn't go to navy for two years.

July 28

We left Long Beach at 7:00 a.m. The sea was quite rough. It seemed more like the Atlantic than the Pacific. Saw movie tonight, *The Castilian*.

July 29

Tony on the Patch

The sea is still rough. Temperature about fifty degrees, it was too cold to go on deck today. I saw a bloke picture tonight, *Escape by Night*. Will this voyage never end?

July 30

Had KP for eight hours today. Ate good though. Saw movie *McLintock* with Tony tonight. He fell asleep during movie.

July 31

Getting a little warmer today. Tony and I went to communion today. Hope our souls are worth saving. Played 500 Rummy with Belmont and lost. About two weeks to go.

August

August 1

Today was pretty boring. Sat on deck all day and read more of my book *Armageddon*. Saw movie *Ride a Pale Horse* at night.

August 2

Had KP today and ate pretty well. Saw movie *Two on a Seesaw*. Was pretty good for a change. Cut myself to ribbons shaving… "Medic, medic!"

August 3

Today water is pretty rough. Atlantic was calmer. Saw good movie tonight, *To Kill a Man*. About marine in VN propaganda?

August 4

Skipped today, crossed international dateline.

August 5

Tony with Author

Sea was really rough today. Saw old calvary movie tonight with Guy Madison. About eight or seven days to go until we land in Cam Ranh Bay, Vietnam.

August 6

Had KP today for five hours but ate most of the time. We are expected to hit part of Typhoon Rita. Temperature is getting warmer.

August 7

Went to mass today on deck. *Rita* hit tonight. Waves were so high; they came over the boat. Quite a few of us got saltwater baths from it.

August 8

Today, just normal. Getting nearer our destination. Tony and I took some pictures tonight. I'm sending them home. It's getting quite a bit warmer.

August 9

Had KP today. Played cards at early night with Belmont; Water is real calm. We passed Iwo Jima at 0200. Distance of about twenty miles.

August 10

Had KP in morning. We are expecting to land on Saturday. Beautiful on deck tonight. Saw part of a picture, *Goliath and the Zombies.*

August 11

Pretty interesting day. Passed Formosa, Manila, Luzon, and a few other small islands. We will land Saturday at *Vũng Tàu*, south of Saigon.

August 12

Had KP all day and saw a movie at night with Tony, name was *40 Pounds of Trouble*. Tomorrow we land at port of debarkation.

August 13

We saw VN at about three o'clock, found out where we will be, Tay Ninh. It is in the lowlands near Cambodia. Not too dangerous; we will fly C-130s to place.

August 14

We got up at 3:00 a.m. Left ship on landing craft at ten o'clock. Boarded C-130s to base camp. Got pretty well set up. Squad tents on cots. Pretty safe artillery and mortars harass enemy.

August 15

Chinook Helo

We are ten miles away from Cambodia and fifty miles from Saigon. Built bunkers near tents. We put equipment on VN oxen carts for easy going. They take cigs. Walked guard last night.

August 16

Got the morning off for guard the night before. We were supposed to go on a patrol, but we built sandbag bunkers instead. The heat is really getting to me.

August 17

Worked most of the day on bunkers. They are used in case of mortar fire. Filipino rangers came in today. They are as small as the Vietnamese soldiers.

August 18

We walked perimeter patrol today. Plenty of "Boom-boom" from Vietnamese women. Kids really like the GIs. Had some 33 beer. It's pretty strong. Had beer in camp at night.

August 19

Today we went on an out of perimeter patrol. Had a lot of fun with the children. They like *Catholic medals*. They are all Catholic.

August 20

Loaded ammo on to choppers. Had action at night. VC hit us with mortars and sniper fire. Two killed from Eighty-Second Arty, three wounded, four BN 31st INF. We weren't hit at all.

August 21

Out on perimeter patrol today. Looked for mines and booby traps. Walked guard at night with Rimassa. No action from VC tonight, glad they took a break.

August 22

Loaded sandbags most of day. At night, "Charlie" planted two claymore mines near one bunker. Bunker detail couldn't get permission to shoot them. *Screw brigade*. Two bunkers fired at each other by mistake.

August 23

Hardest workday. Loaded sandbags and strung barbed wire. Walked guard at night. Recon sent out ambush patrol. Fired on VC but no hits. I didn't make this patrol, Bun Qua (sorry about that).

August 24

Had perimeter patrol this morning. Went to spot of last night's ambush. Found magazine plus first aid pouch someone dropped. At night, suspected VC in camp. On alert in bunker until 12:00 p.m. Went to bed.

August 25

Went out on a four-thousand-meter patrol today. Found nothing. They moved a company of montagnards into the rubber plantation near us. Ambush patrol went out. Found nothing. I stayed back.

August 26

Crushed and punctured cans this morning. VC make bombs out of them if they are intact. Went out on perimeter patrol in afternoon. *Carried PRC-25 radio*, slept well. No night action.

August 27

Went on two patrols today on fence. I carried radio twice. Worked until about 7:00 p.m. Had beer at night. Quiet night. No action from VC.

August 28

Worked half a day today. Got paid two months' pay. Relaxed most of night and caught up on some of my mail. First day, we got a whole afternoon off.

August 29

Worked on sandbags all morning. Relaxed some of the afternoon. Patrol at night. Didn't see anything. It rained all night. Pretty chilly.

August 30

Had day off because of ambush detail. A Company and B Company went out after large force of VC. *VC got out.* No action reported. Got short haircut at night.

August 31

Carried sandbags most of the day. Worked on cutting grass the afternoon. Nothing exciting. VC are pretty quiet.

September

September 1

Cut grass in field to clear fields of fire. *Captain Gregg* had us pulling up roots for Vietnamese farmers. He said, "Don't ever talk to Viet people." He broke his own rule.

September 2

Cao Dai Temple

Captain Gregg left company, went to "A" company. We now have Captain Leeds. Seems all right.

Had bunker detail at night since "B" and "C" company out on operation. No Action.

September 3

Today is Sunday. We had most of day off. Had some Bier Larue at night. Two of them is enough to knock you out. *"C" company 3/21* lost one man and two wounded in *operation "Allan."*

September 4

Went out on seven-mile patrol along highway 13. Have to secure road for coming elections. Had a little sniper fire at night. No big thing. *Gumba* and "B" company came in after three days.

September 5

Correction. I lost one day somewhere. Today's message is the same as yesterday, Bung Qua.

September 6

Had sandbag detail in morning. Rested all afternoon for *Eagle Flight* the next day. Had two bottles of Bier Larue tonight.

September 7

Had *Eagle Flight* mission in daytime until about 1:00 p.m. Found nothing but old tunnels. Had bunkers at night. Nothing unusual. Busy day and night.

September 8

Go *on* bunkers in early morning. Had guard at night. Belmont accidentally shot Sergeant Burris of "A" company. He is in good shape though. Hope Belmont doesn't get hit hard.

September 9

Got half a day off for having guard. Rested all of afternoon. Had ambush patrol at night 4,800 meters out. No action but hostile mosquitos.

September 10

Had day off for patrol previous night. Got a lot of *Zs*. Had to stay awake four hours at night in preparation for any election hostilities.

September 11

In morning, we built some makeshift shelves for our stuff in the tents. In afternoon, had practice alert inspection. No action at night from VC.

September 12

Had KP today. A big blantz. Work on pots and pans all afternoon until seven thirty at night. Really dirty job. Went to CP. Helped Holly and *Brede* sing "Black Beret."

September 13

Had bunkers all day and night. At night, we spotted figures out in front of us in cemetery. *Sergeant Rich* fired 2–12 gauge shells. No hits.

September 14

Had morning off because of bunker detail. Loaded sandbags in afternoon. Had guard at night. We moved our tents today. No floors yet.

September 15

Went to Tây Ninh today for laundry and some things. Town is old like a bazaar. Finally got lamp and footlocker. Had mucho beer at night. Copped little *high*.

Dusty Ride

September 16

Worked on water drainage ditch all day. Drank plenty of beer. Had to stay up one hour for alert guard.

September 17

Had 5,100-meter patrol, which actually was longer because of Looey's stupid mistakes. Had most of late afternoon and night off. No rain for once.

September 18

Head very big from massive party night before. Throat rasp. Parched. I'll survive, however. Had bunkers at night. Nothing unusual. Throat getting better.

September 19

Had morning off for bunkers night before. Worked in afternoon on sandbags; we had the night off for once. Played a little catch and jammed shoulder.

September 20

Had pretty easy morning. Was supposed to put up fence in morning, but fence never arrived. Dug rain ditch in afternoon and evening.

September 21

Had to dig rain ditch in morning. Started on wooden floor for tent in afternoon. Had bunkers at night. Nothing unusual.

September 22

Had morning off. Well, we finally got wood floors and screen doors. Just like a summer cottage. Much more comfortable. Worked until dark on rain ditch.

September 23

Worked on rain ditch and bunker wall for tent. No rain today for a change. Had night off and read part of *Kon-Tiki*. Got to sleep about 1:00 a.m.

September 24

Had fence patrol today and a party. Had 33 beer and talked plus learned Vietnamese. Met fifteen-year-old boy in high school. Gave him dictionary. Had bunkers at night. No action.

September 25

Had morning off. Put up another fence in afternoon. Another obstacle for Charlie. Had colossal party at night. Poured beer all over squad leader, Arivett.

September 26

Had morning off. In afternoon, worked on new fence in between existing two. Nothing at night. Didn't get to sleep until about one thirty.

September 27

Worked on fence in morning. Rode shotgun for trucks picking up "A" company about ten miles other side of mountain. Had bunkers at night.

September 28

Had morning off, wrote letters. In afternoon, had some beer for *Marler's* birthday. Had trash detail. Had cake and beer at night at *Marler's* party.

September 29

Built a house for officer's tent today. Hope it stays up, it isn't too secure. Nothing to do at night, so I just wrote letters.

September 30

Had small *work* detail in morning, got paid today. Moved shower near well, running water from pump. Had bunkers at night. No action. Moon very bright.

October

October 1

Went into town today. Picked up gifts for home. Bought watch for $11, pretty good buy. Took some pictures of girls in Johnny's laundry; quiet night.

October 2

Worked on ditch in morning and afternoon. At night, guarded road near villages. Had party of *C-Rats* and beer after guard. 1:00 a.m.

Tay NinhCity

October 3

Worked in morning and had bunkers at night. *Sergeant Brown* left pistol belt at *LP* when they pulled in because of rain. *VC took grenade; Stout got hit with shrapnel from VC.*

October 4

Had morning off. Put up concertina in afternoon. Rest of time to prepare for search and destroy mission tomorrow. Sorry about that.

October 5

We had mission today and through to tomorrow. Had patrol and found abandoned VC *camp*. Exploded some dud bombs from our *planes*; pretty quiet at night.

October 6

Came in from mission today about 11:00 a.m., had rest of the day off to rest. "B" company relieved us and as of the 7th, had six wounded and one dead, must be lucky.

October 7

We had to work on trench and area today, burned latrine kettles, got another parrot, hope this one doesn't get away. We go out tomorrow *indefinitely*.

Viet Good Humor Kid

October 8

Went out on ambush patrol today. Went with "A" company to our spot. Rested in concealment for day. As it grew dark, took up spots. Howe and me North LP; starlight works okay.

October 9

Nothing happened night before. Left for base at about 10:00 a.m. Had rest of day off. Got some mail and am answering it. 175-mm *howitzer* kept us awake.

October 10

Had bunkers all day, so had a lot of rest. On bunker 1 at night, drank beer with MPs. Strange light on road. No action.

October 11

Had morning off and mailed some packages; had afternoon off to prepare for coming mission. Have to wake up at 3:30 a.m.

October 12

Left for operation North Star with Lt. Col Happersatt, leading. Good dude. Special forces CO securing for 106s. Blew caves, bridges, went back to VN camp fortnight.

On the Way to Nui Ba Den

October 13

Went out farther on road around mountain. Burned huts, caves. Encountered sniper fire. No casualties. *CIB A-go-go. Came in about 1:00 a.m. Soothe.*

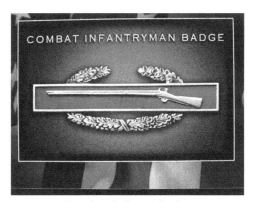

Combat Infantry Badge

October 14

Worked all day on company arena. Learned that we won't be going out on 15th. *With line company's* tomorrow. Somebody gave us a break.

October 15

Went to bunkers in morning but had to come back. Line companies went out. Had LP tonight on bunkers. Nobody to be seen.

October 16

Had day off for once. Guess we earned it. Had 1,500-meter squad ambush at night. Moore and me *had* spot. No action, except for *ARVN spotlight.*

October 17

Had day off for ambush the night before. Bunkers tonight, but I have KP. Sorry about that. Charlie exploded *charge* in front of bunker 4. No one hurt.

October 18

Had KP today. What a blantz. *Sp/5 Watkins* slave driver. Not a break all day. Rain and monsoons all night. Miserable.

October 19

Worked on trench bunker all day. Almost finished now. Used all sandbags up, so had big break in afternoon. Had guard at night.

October 20

Had some of morning off for guard. Saw Martha Raye and two musicians in show. Pretty good. For old lady. Had LP tonight but came in at 1:00 a.m. Too much rain.

Martha Ray Performing in Tay Ninh

October 21

Had morning off for LP night before. Went on fence patrol in afternoon; MPs chased people away. They came back though. Had night off.

October 22

Had trash detail in morning and early afternoon. Vietnamese unloaded all trash. They use most of it. Had bunkers at night, no action.

Author with Viet Kids

October 23

Had off until 9:00 a.m. Had work on trench around tent. Finished trench and built small bunker in front of tent. Had afternoon off and pitched horseshoes.

October 24

Had bunkers during day; *General. Desesaurus* came to inspect. Pretty nice guy. Got chewed out by Captain Chew for not saluting. Had bunkers at night. Nothing unusual.

October 25

Had morning off and afternoon until 4:00 p.m. Went on two-night ambush patrol. Went about three thousand meters for first ambush. Nothing to be seen. Mucho mosquitos.

October 26

Went to next ambush sight about two thousand meters from first one. Rested during the day. Couldn't handle no sleep. Fell asleep about 6:00 a.m. No one to be seen. Two companies of VC supposedly here.

October 27

Got back to camp about 1:00 p.m. Had rest of day off. Good to sleep in own cots for a change. Went to sleep about nine o'clock and rested peacefully at night.

October 28

Had trash detail in the morning. Blantz. Cooks push you until you can't go anymore. Had bunkers at night with Rimassa and Roseberry. Nothing unusual.

October 29

Cleaned out tent in morning and went to town with company in afternoon. Picked up presents for Dad and Bob. Played volleyball at late evening.

October 30

Had to finish off bunker wall in back of tent. Worked a little on horseshoe pit. Had guard at night, saw television. Sound not good. Candid camera was on.

October 31

Halloween. Went on three-day ambush patrol today. Walked from 4:30 p.m. to 10:30 p.m. in pouring rain through rice paddies. Blantz. Trick or treat. Spent rest of night in soggy ambush. No action.

November

***

November 1

Rested during day. Went to get water from rice paddy with Bushers, Moore, Lizotte, Miller and Sharp on LP. Snipers fired on us. We fired back and brought in artillery. No action at night.

November 2

Came back into camp tired as ever. Had day off to rest up a little. Watched a little TV tonight. "C" company lost one man on *counter* ambush tonight.

November 3

Worked on fence in morning. Had ambush patrol at night. VC hit camp with mortars; we were two thousand meters from VC mortar position. One major, lieutenant killed, fifty-seven wounded near eighth support. VC used soviet mortars.

November 4

Had morning off. Had another ambush patrol at night. No action. VC mortared laterite pits. "C" company *3/21*, ten killed, two platoons wounded by Boi Loi Woods. Hardcore.

November 5

Went to Boi Loi Woods today with brigade. Had some fire. Big Red One moved in also. Slept pretty good as *Col's* security.

November 6

Went into Boi Loi. Found dead VC and dead GIs. Set up perimeter in woods at night. Attack by VC of *rifle*-grenades at night.

November 7

Went into another part of Boi Loi. Hit with claymores. Miller and *Green* hit. We retreated and set up perimeter. No action at night.

November 8

Went little way into woods. Sharp and I *on LP*; Claymore goes off and we retreat again. We *go to Qua Trang.* Big red; 1 supply base.

November 9

Go on patrol A, B company. Stay on defensive perimeter. We had bunkers at night. Fell asleep, though choppers came in most of night.

November 10

Battalion went on patrol, but I guarded equipment near base. Came back to base camp by C-123s. Good to sleep in bunks.

November 11

Had day off to clean up gear, etc. Went over to "B" company for some good chow. We were hit twice with mortars during night. Our battalion wasn't hit.

November 12

Went on fence patrol today and had a few drinks, had bunkers at night. Intelligence reported a VC human wave attack due for tonight. Nothing *doing*.

November 13

Worked on fence until three o'clock in the afternoon. Had to go in swamp up to waist. Blantz! Had rest of day off. Bought Bowie knife. Had guard at night.

November 14

Had off until about 10:00 a.m. Platoon went on Eagle Flight in afternoon; I stayed back. Had bunkers at night. No action.

November 15

Had off until about eight thirty. Had to relieve *Mac* on bunker 8. He got sick. Read part of a book. Easy day, had off at night, played some records.

November 16

Went to laterite pit all day. Met two Vietnamese girls, Mai (seventeen), Lien (fifteen). Drank plenty of coke. Talked to Filipinos. Had night off. Rimassa in *pup tent* for a week. Sorry about that.

November 17

Worked on area. Painted hooch up. Had bunker 1 at night. Lot of action at 3 and 4. Rifle-grenades came in. Had some beer and listened to records with *MPs*.

November 18

Had day off from night before. Mailed package down at brigade. Rode security for trucks, bearing ambush patrol. Had some beer at night. Good sleep.

November 19

Went to laterite today. Talked with Filipinos Got pictures from Lien Watched a little TV. "C" Co. got ambushed going on ambush.

November 20

Had trash detail today. Went out 2:00 p.m. to ambush site for night; near "C" company was ambushed last night. No action.

November 21

Had day off. Just lounged around and wrote letters. Had bunkers at night with 8/th. Support LP fired at VC. No hits. One chopper downed at laterite pit.

November 22

Worked on tent all day. Did a little painting. Watched TV at night, *Rawhide*. There was movie, *Madame X*. No good. Quiet and chilly night.

November 23

Had battalion trash run today. Worked on wash-stands in afternoon. Saw movie *The Americanization of Emily*. Real good.

November 24

Had bunkers all day. Happy Thanksgiving. Got sick and got off bunkers at night. Had turkey for supper meal. Peaceful night.

November 25

Worked on squad area. Painted washstand. Worked on squad bunker in back of tent. Played some volleyball. Baseball game for movie. Blantz. Quiet night.

November 26

Worked on squad bunker. Fired our weapons late afternoon. Filipino *Guantanamos* came over to tent. Gave him old boots. Slept peacefully at night.

November 27

Went to town today and picked up some goodies and went to Johnie's laundry. Have KP tomorrow, so I beat bunkers tonight.

November 28

Had KP today until about 10:00 a.m. Left about two o'clock for ambush patrol. Rained twice. Buku uncomfortable. Only thing we saw, stray animal.

November 29

Had off all day but had another ambush at night. Rained all night. Big blantz. *Kettles* hit in knee with shrapnel from Stout's M79 by accident.

November 30

Had day off for ambush night before. Didn't sleep though. Listened to records. Had another ambush at night, three for three. No action.

December

***

December 1

Had day off for ambush the night before. Rested all day and played some volleyball. Slept in cots for once. Have KP tomorrow.

December 2

Had KP today, *was DRO*. Not too bad. Got off at six thirty. Battalion went out near Cambodia today, possibly for twenty days. Went to bed at 10:00 p.m. Peaceful night.

December 3

Had morning off for once. Had laterite all afternoon, bought some odds and ends. Had guard at night with Hoop. Pretty chilly but quiet.

December 4

Had to work for short time in morning. Had afternoon at laterite. Pretty hot. Had night off for once, wrote letters and listened to records.

December 5

Had day off to prepare for ambush at night. Went to Lan's Laundry and had some beer. Almost got caught. Quiet night on ambush.

December 6

Had day off for ambush night before. Had LP on bunkers at night. It rained about nine thirty. We came in. *Beat it four times in row.*

December 7

Had day off because had *roving* ambush patrol at night. Left at nine o'clock and had to move to two positions. Don't like idea. No action.

December 8

Had most of day off because of ambush previous night. Had bunkers at night. VC supposed to hit ARVN post. Nothing happened.

December 9

Had off till nine o'clock then had to work on BTOC bunker until eleven o'clock. Went to laterite pit in afternoon. Slept in bunks at night. For once.

December 10

Had laterite in morning. Had afternoon off but had bunkers. Slept all night in bunker 1, MPs kept awake. Rick Way shot a flare off. No action.

December 11

Had off till nine o'clock then had to work on ground for basketball court. Went to laterite afternoon. Lien in Cu Chi, but left note and medal for me. On thirty-minute alert but didn't go out.

December 12

Went out by chopper for *S and D ambush* at night. Put up ambush near house in jungle. Rabbit jumped on me. Quite frightening. No action.

December 13

Got resupplied by chopper. Had to stay out until four o'clock. Rested most of the day. Tony *Sciavolino* killed by accident on ambush. "B" company go on *R+R* Friday.

December 14

Had morning off. Supposed to go on ambush but canceled. Played volleyball in afternoon. Slept in bunkers at night. Two nights in row.

December 15

Had bunkers all day with Sharp. Recon went out on ambush at night. Didn't make this one.

December 16

Took C-123 to camp ALPHA (Tan Son Nhut Airfield). Spent time playing slot machines. No luck. Slept in bunks. Pretty comfortable.

December 17

Waited until 5:00 p.m. for flight to Philippines. Landed about 10:20 p.m. Got room (Sharp-Jones-me) in Sampaguita Hotel. Slept well, but not alone.

December 18

First day in Manila. Went to see WWII Memorial cemetery. Rode past millionaire acres. Have bad cold but handled another night.

December 19

Went shopping and saw good movie, *Dr. Zhivago*. Also went to Sangley Point-Naval Base. Very peaceful sleep at night.

December 20

Saw another movie today, *The Blue Max*. Real good. Went to *Goliath's*. Restless night, have cold from air conditioner.

December 21

Had to go back out to Sangley Point to exchange tape recorder Don bought. Went to places of interest. Stopped at Sally's. Good night. Slept well, but not alone.

December 22

Woke up at four thirty. Had to be at R+R center at five thirty. Left for Vietnam. Arrived at twelve thirty and spent night at Camp Alpha. Good sleep.

December 23

Rode C-123 to Tay-Ninh, arrived about 11:30 a.m. Went out on three-day mission with company at three o'clock. Nice welcome-home surprise. Had ambush at night. Quiet.

December 24

Went on short patrol today and moved with company to new location. Had perimeter guard at night. Eight reindeers and one fat man reported in the area. Quiet eve.

December 25

Came back into camp about 10:00 a.m. Had a turkey dinner, not bad. EM Club opened. Had all free booze and beer. Pretty good time. Plenty of "big" heads.

December 26

Had bunker duty all day with Sharp. Didn't have bunkers at night because of ambush tomorrow night. Saw *Red Line 7000* at movie.

December 27

Had off all day for ambush preparation. Caught up on most of my mail. Left at 3:30 p.m. for ambush. Quiet night as usual.

December 28

Had off all day because of ambush night before. Had bunkers at night with Way and Kettles. Pretty cold, almost froze. Slept pretty good though.

December 29

Had trash detail in morning. Goofed off all afternoon. Had bunkers with *Mortars*. We are losing guys to 2/27 Wolfhounds.

December 30

Had laterite all day. Saw little Lien last night; for guys leaving: Sharp, McFarland, Shiffer, Hoop, Moore, Roseberry, Myers, Marrero, Green, and Kline. Hate to see them go.

December 31

Had morning off but had to go out in afternoon. Got hit with claymore and rifle grenades at night. Not too peaceful. A cease-fire.

January

January 1

Had day off and came in. Went to EM Club during day. Got a few more new guys today. Had guard with Maxwell at night.

January 2

Went down to PX in morning and bought new 35mm camera. Beat bunkers at night and also KP. I was supposed to have peaceful sleep.

January 1

Had day off and came in. went to EM Club during day. Got a few more new guys today. Had guard with Maxwell at night.

January 3

Had bunkers during the day. Took some pictures with new camera. Had bunker 4 with *Bundy and Florence*, shot flare up just for fun.

January 4

Had day off because of ambush tonight. Brought new guys out on ambush. I'm point man for first squad. Cold but quiet night.

January 5

Had off for ambush night before. Bought bottle of Seagram's 7. Good for party. Have KP tomorrow. Had a few beers in EM Club.

January 6

Had KP today so got up at four thirty. Got stuck on pots and pans anyway. Brigade went out on operation today. We stayed back. *Single*.

January 7

Went out to laterite today. Stayed out all day. Took some pictures, had some beer in EM Club, had guard at night with *Bundy*.

January 8

Had day off so went to PX and bought new suitcase. Had ambush tonight. I'm point man now. Peaceful night.

January 9

Had most of day off, except for having bunkers at night. Had LP. Got chance to stop in EM Club. Some grenades thrown, otherwise quiet.

January 10

Went out to laterite pit all during day. Had night off, so went down to *PHILCAG* camp with *Bundy*. Had a real swell party.

January 11

Had laterite until noon. Had "head" from last night. Had ambush at night. Had some sleep. Found cobra in second squad drain ditch today.

January 12

Had most of day off because of ambush night before. Worked on fence in afternoon. Beat bunkers tonight. Saw *Our Man Flint* on movie.

January 13

Had fence in morning but put on alert. Charlie mortared PHILCAG on road. Up most of night. Charlie kept us awake. Slept outside tent near bunker.

January 14

Had to go on road security in morning. Rest up for ambush at night. Quiet night on ambush. Camp hit last night. ARVN post hit tonight.

January 15

Had off until afternoon. Had to work on fence until 3:30 p.m. Went on bunkers tonight. Took some pictures with *Konica*. Quiet night.

January 16

Had to work on fence in morning. In afternoon, had to go to laterite in afternoon, had night off, except for alert at seven thirty. Hassle.

January 17

Had to go laterite in morning. Bought buku cookies from Lien. Had ambush at night. Pretty cold. Had LP with *Savedo*. Not much action except shivering.

January 18

Had day off until afternoon. Had to work on fence. Came back at 3:00 p.m. to go on bunkers. Quiet night. Larry Myers killed recently with "C" company 2/27.

January 19

Had morning off after bunkers night before. In afternoon, out to laterite again. Bought buku cokes. Real muggy day. Saw *Queen of Blood* at night.

January 20

Went out to laterite pit in morning. Sometimes, kids a nuisance. Had CQ at night with Miller. Had fast night. Slept a little.

January 21

Had off today because of CQ night before, slept most of day. On bunkers for one hour because *Way and Rauvala* high on pot. Came back for KP in morning.

January 22

Had KP all day, not too bad, *DRO* got off early at 6:15 p.m. Filipinos came up tonight. Had real good time until about twelve o'clock. Had to sack out. Buku tired.

January 23

Had road security today. Plenty of kids out there. Had afternoon off for ambush at night. Rained until 10:00 p.m. Miller and me on LP. Quiet night.

January 24

Had morning off and went to Philippines and US PX. Goofed off in afternoon. Had to go on bunkers at night. On bunker 1. Quiet.

January 25

Had off till nine o'clock, had to work on bunker until eleven o'clock. Buku num qua. Went on laterite in afternoon. Had night off. Slept well until alert.

January 26

Had road security during morning. Had afternoon off for ambush at night. Battalion came in today. Bright and quiet night.

January 27

Had most of day off, except for small harassing details. Had party at night in club. PHILCAG came up. Usual gang. Went to bed about one o'clock.

January 28

Had laterite in morning. Had to work until three o'clock on fence. Had LP (bunker) at night. Sixty incoming mortars hit camp. No casualties. "C" company hit with friendly artillery. Three killed, eight wounded.

January 29

Had morning off and went to church services. Had to go to laterite in afternoon. Fired a few magazines. Drank some beer and went to sleep.

January 30

Went out on three-day two-night ambush patrol at four o'clock. Got to sight at dark. Had to move though. Miller saw three VC but no permission to fire.

January 31

Went on short S-and-D mission. Had trail day watch. Rested until night. Went to ambush position. Pretty thick but quiet night.

February

February 1

Came in today from ambush patrol. Went to PX twice today. Had tonight off, so got pretty drunk. Had ice cream and beer and went to sleep.

February 2

Had KP today on pots and pans. Hassle. Didn't work too hard though. Got off about seven thirty. Had a few beers and played records at EM Club.

February 3

Went out on two-night ambush patrol. Took two scout dogs out into *AO-2*. Moved slow with dogs. Got to spot. No action.

February 4

Moved few thousand meters on S-and-D mission. Set up ambush at night. On LP with scout dog. Dog too noisy. One VC spotted. No shooting.

February 5

Had day off when we returned. Slept most of day. Filipinos came up night to help me celebrate birthday. Great bunch of guys.

February 6

Had laterite all day today. Saw picture *Harum Scarum* at night. "B" company, one killed on mountain tonight. Little action on bubble tonight.

February 7

Went out on ambush today at three thirty. Saw one VC at eleven thirty, one incoming grenade, fired back but with no results. No more action at night.

February 8

Rested for tonight's ambush but called in. Had to go out with "A" company to secure bunkers near Suoi Da, pretty quiet here, and a lot of rest.

February 9

Had a restful day. Had nothing to do all day but sleep. Had a little of that. Had same bunker tonight. Really quiet.

February 10

Had another restful day, except for small patrol. Had bunkers again at night. Fell asleep as usual but not caught.

February 11

Had about a ten-thousand-meter patrol. Real hassle. Crossed a small river. Just about made it back. Gregg breaking our back with all the patrols. No Charlies.

February 12

Went on about a fourteen-thousand-meter patrol with a platoon from "A" company. We swept a three-thousand-meter area while "A" Company Plt. was blocking force. Worse patrol in Vietnam. No action.

February 13

Went into camp today for resupply. Got a break from a patrol. Came back at four o'clock. Pulled bunkers as usual.

February 14

Went out on another *sweep* operation today. "A" Company Plt. sat down as blocking force as usual. Got one prisoner with buku money. Maybe VC paymaster.

February 15

Went out by chopper about eight thousand meters. Walked flank for "A" Company Plt. Hassle. Sergeant Mayfield found drum of rice. Blew it up. Long walk back in. Real tired.

February 16

Went out on our own patrol. Not too bad. Burned buku brush. Came in early. Jeep in convoy hit mine. Thought I saw something at night, only paper.

February 17

Had the day off for once. Rested up and read some of *Goldfinger*. Had bunkers at night as usual. Tomorrow we will go back to camp.

February 18

Had small heliborne mission then went back to base camp. We are to be a line company. Not too different from what we are doing now.

February 19

Had most of day off today. Got a haircut. Got another new camera: Yashica-Mat double-reflex. Real nice. Saw *Pleasure Seekers* at night.

February 20

Had most of today off. Moved into the mortar tents. Had to get two shots today. I'm "B" team leader now. Drank some beer and sweet dreams.

February 21

Had M16 class today like I really need it. Supposed to fire weapons today but have to go on ambush instead. Quiet night.

February 22

Had day off but have to go on another ambush tonight. Moved into mortar tents. A, B, C Company hit hot *LZs on* mission. Some casualties.

February 23

Had off today, so went out and bought new radio. Panasonic all transistor. Had to go to laterite at night. Nice and quiet. Not much sleep.

February 24

Had laterite in afternoon. Came back in and had night off for once. Watched movie. Went to bed early but to sleep late. Noisy guys.

February 25

Went to laterite in morning and had ambush at night. Moon out, so very bright. Lost CS grenade, too bad.

February 26

Had day off, so went to PX. Getting warmer. Have to go to laterite at night. It rained about thirty minutes. Very rare.

February 27

Had day off again. Rather have night off though. Had ambush at night. Stray shot from ARVN outpost too close for comfort.

February 28

Had day off again but too hot to sleep. Had laterite at night, saw Lien back from Cu Chi. Quiet night.

February 29

No leap year, sorry about that.

March
———

March 1

Had day off. Supposed to play "D" company 4/31 in volleyball, but they didn't make it, one win. Had ambush at night, quiet as usual.

March 2

Had off during the day as usual. Slept a few hours. Have another ambush tonight. One VC *seen* last night by LP. Lot of firing but no *VC*.

March 3

Had off all day as usual. Got about three hours sleep under the influence of beer. Went on about three-thousand-meter ambush. Quiet night.

March 4

Went out to Nui Ba Den for security on rock quarry. Really close to mountain. Slept well. Good chow from "F" troop.

March 5

On the Way to Nui Ba Den

Came back in from the mountain about 1:00 p.m. Had day off to straighten up. Had some drinks and slept well at night.

March 6

Had day off, which is unusual since we didn't have an ambush last night. Went for a walk to the PX. Had an ambush tonight. Hard time staying awake.

March 7

Had day off for ambush night before. Went to both PXs and goofed off most of day. Went down to PHILCAG at night to visit the boys.

March 8

Had to dig ditch near *BOQ*. Hassle. Had inspection in afternoon. Had laterite at night. Saw Lien too. Peaceful night.

March 9

Beat work in morning, hid and wrote letters. Rested most of afternoon for ambush at night. Rained a little but quiet.

March 10

Had day off for ambush night before. Went to PHICAG, and drank and ate heartily. On bunker LP at night. Buford threw T-flare to try and wake us. Hot seat.

March 11

Had off supposedly until noon but beat the entire day. Some of the Filipino boys came up at night. Had a pretty good night.

March 12

Went out to road security by Nui Ba Den all day. Had night off, so went to PHILCAG. *SP/5* Gregg paid us a drunken visit at 1:00 a.m. Got a bottle for free.

March 13

Went out on road security in morning near mountain. Came in in afternoon for ambush. Bought new *Miranda* camera at PX. Burch threw grenade in ambush.

March 14

Had day off for ambush night before. Had bunkers at night. Saw two Huey's collide rotor blades while on ground. No serious casualties.

March 15

Had day off but had to go on "bubble" bunkers tonight. Really secure, lighted up. Have to go out *A-O-BLUE* tomorrow. Don't know how long.

March 16

We came out to A-O-BLUE today for about a week. Security for artillery battery. Had ambush in rubber tonight, but quiet.

March 17

Had to walk highway for mine detection. Took all day. didn't find anything. Pulled bunkers at night as usual. Quiet.

March 18

Went out to pull security on first bridge today. Buku boom-boom and coke a fold. Had bunkers at night as usual. Quiet.

March 19

Had short patrol and practiced squad assaults. Back to school. Had to go on about three-thousand-meter ambush patrol tonight in rubber (stupid place). No action.

March 20

Had to sweep short portion of road for mines. Rested by second bridge most of morning. Came back and rested in afternoon. Quiet night.

March 21

Had to sweep for mines this morning, had afternoon off. Expected to be *overrun* at night but never happened. VC regiment near. Quiet night.

March 22

Had day off, so rested up. Too hot to sleep. Had to go on ambush at night near *two thousand* bridge. Quiet, except for bats and mosquitoes.

March 23

Went back to base camp this afternoon. Had night off for once and slept soundly. Alcohol helped though. *One hundred thirteen days left until return home.*

March 24

Had to prepare for equipment inspection, which never came. Bought new 35mm Canon camera. Had bunkers at night. Plenty of sleep.

March 25

Came back out to A-O-BLUE. Have to keep people away from camp. Have real nice bunkers. Moon out at night and real quiet.

March 26

Went into base camp on resupply. Went in with artillery convoy. Got lost but made it. Drank buku beer, had bunkers at night as usual.

March 27

Had most of day off. Pretty odd for Easter Sunday. Have to go on roving ambush tonight in rubber. No contact though.

March 28

Had day off and got some sleep in the afternoon. Had bunker guard as usual. Slept pretty soundly though. LP out to front.

March 29

Had day off but didn't get much sleep. Went down to road and bought cokes from kids. Had bunkers at night as usual.

March 30

Went on patrol today and searched rubber plantation houses. Nothing to be found. Went back to base camp in afternoon. Had night off and got drunk.

March 31

Had morning off and got paid. Went down PX and bought new watch. Had to go out to laterite pit at night. Saw Lien and bought some shirts.

April

April 1

Stayed out in laterite till afternoon. Rode motorbike. Went out to Nui Ba Den late afternoon. "A" company: eight killed, two wounded out in A-O-BLUE on mine-sweep detail. *Sergeant Press* one of them.

Lien and Mai at AO-2

April 2

Spent most of day building bunker. Pretty hot but plenty of beer to drink. Drove jeep a little. Had bunkers at night as usual.

April 3

Had most of day off because have ambush tonight. Got plenty of rest. Went out about 1,600 meters on ambush near stream. Quiet and no mosquitoes.

April 4

Had morning off but had to work some on bunkers in afternoon. Had small monsoon at night. All bunkers flooded except ours. Slept outside tonight.

April 5

Had to pull road security for engineers on main road. Supposed to go up north with battalion today but didn't go. Maybe tomorrow. Quiet night, except for H+I.

April 6

Viet Kids at AO-2

Had day off and tried to sleep but to no avail. Had ambush tonight. Two VC spotted but got away. Williams landed HE round about fifteen feet away from Miller and me. Too close for comfort.

April 7

Had day off again but couldn't sleep. Had *Mad-Minute*, which was set off by some trigger-happy idiot. Four in bunker, so had buku sleep. Quiet.

April 8

Came back in to base camp in afternoon. Have to pack tonight, brigade moving out to Chu Lai, attached to marines. Hassle, have to pick up everything.

April 9

Got up at 4:30 a.m. Left Tay Ninh sat 6:00 p.m. One and a half hour flight. Got to Chu Lai at seven forty-five and sacked out for night. We'll know where we'll be stationed tomorrow.

April 10

Pulled security in hills during day and in field all afternoon. Went to our "mountain" base camp in evening. All hills. Slept on wood floor; don't have tents yet.

April 11

Had to go on some harassment details during day. Had to go on bunkers at night. Beautiful off hill. Plenty of firefights in distance.

Monsoon Rain

April 12

Had most of day off. Had ambush at night, not too far out. Chu Lai airfield got hit with mortars last night. Lietz slept all night. Had to endure sleeplessness.

April 13

Had morning off but had to go on 4,200-meter patrol. Hills make you real tired. Had night off, so went to movie. Not enough electricity for movie. Rainy night.

Author on Combat Patrol

April 14

Had to go to *OP-7* all day. Vietnamese understand English better here than Tay Ninh. Stayed at night but had eight men in bunker. No sweat.

Combat Patrol in "I" Corps.

April 15

Had off most of the day, beat detail. In a few days, we'll be allowed to go to beach. Can't wait. Had ambush at night, quiet.

April 16

Had day off, so rested and played some catch with football. Played a little basketball at evening. Watched *Man from U.N.C.L.E.* film at night. Peaceful.

April 17

Had all day off, so just rested and goofed off. Had bunkers at night. Not too bad, three in a bunker. Quiet as usual.

Author with 60mm Mortar Round

April 18

Had day off, but it rained all the time. Had to go on ambush at night with third squad. Stopped raining, but plenty cold. Quiet.

April 19

Had to go on patrol during day, up and down hills and dales. Had bunkers at night with Miller and Rauvala. Chilly but quiet as usual.

April 20

Went on patrol for most of day. Went through village. Hills and mountains really beat you. Had night off and copped high plus got sick. Sweet dreams.

April 21

Went on patrol with most of company. Buku walking plus *bighead*. Finished *Abortion* about two o'clock and came in. Night off. Two in a row, unbelievable.

April 22

Had patrol that turned out to be VC wild goose chase. ARVNs shot Vietnamese boy, left him to die, should have shot them. Ambush at night, few shots fired at movement.

Author after 10 Kilometer Patrol

April 23

Had all day off, so just rested. Had bunkers at night. Rained most of night. "C" company moved out, so we have rest of bunker line, hassle.

April 24

Had off most of the day and just rested. Pulled bunkers at night with Miller. No top on bunker and it rained. Sorry about that. Moon out but quiet.

April 25

Had hassle police call most of day. Squad ambush at night. Two *volunteer* mutts assumed scout dog roles. Too noisy though.

April 26

Were supposed to go swimming today but had to build bunker instead. Move into new area tomorrow. Had night off for once. Everyone else on bunkers.

April 27

Moved to our new area and had to put up tents with floors. Quite a workout. Had to go on bunkers at night. Slept on hard sandbags.

April 28

On bunkers till about noon, then had to clean up old area. Hassle. Buku beer cans. Had night off, watched *Batman* and Gunsmoke 1.

April 29

Had to go out to OP North at twelve o'clock until twelve o'clock next day. Fish jumping all night. Pretty quiet. Threw one grenade in stream, extent of action.

April 30

Went back into base camp after wading in stream for beer and "C" cans. Real hassle. Had to go on bunkers at night. Not too bad except for "Pyscho Williams."

May

—

May 1

Had bunkers till noon. Had ambush at night. Eighty to ninety VC spotted by "B" company, gunships flew plus flares all night, pretty hairy. Not much sleep to be had. Getting too short for action.

May 2

Came back in from ambush patrol. Had to go on detail but turned out good. Found sandbags and just loaded them on truck, then went to *ROK Club* at night. Beer a fold. Off at night.

May 3

Had to mine sweep highway 1 in morning and pick up old ammo boxes off in afternoon and had platoon ambush at night. Hilly area but quiet.

May 4

Had morning off and went swimming in afternoon. Water and beach beautiful. Went to ROK Club for a few drinks. Almost hassle. Had night off.

May 5

Had morning off. Had to go on bunkers in afternoon with *Bryant*. Stayed in bunkers all night, good music from AFRS, quiet and cool.

Chu Lai Beach

Troops at Chu Lai Beach

Author at Chu Lai Beach

May 6

Stayed on bunker till noon. Beat work in afternoon. Copped small high and went to bunkers at night. "B" company ambushed tonight.

May 7

Had morning off but didn't feel too well. Rested up in afternoon, went out to OP-6 at night. Buku firefight about one thousand meters from us on highway 1.

May 8

Had mine-sweep detail in morning. Went on bunkers in afternoon and at night. Party with Doc and Bryant in 2. Hammock collapsed, and I broke radio in fall.

May 9

Had off all day, which is unusual. Pretty hot today, but beer helped. Had bunkers at night with Rauvala and Bryant. Little chilly out tonight.

May 10

Had to work on bunker in morning. Went to OP-7 in afternoon. Rested up. Had eight at night, so pulled one hour guard. Buku sleep.

May 11

Had morning off and wrote letters. Had interview for radio report with other guys. Had bunkers at night, quiet as usual.

May 12

Had to work in morning, buku hot. Had afternoon off, so just rested and wrote letters. Had ambush at night. Up on booby-trap hill.

May 13

Had off all day and just goofed off. Had to go to OP-6 at night. Bought jacket from *Tom*. ARVNs checked up on us at night. Quiet though.

May 14

Had off in morning. Worked on first squad bunker in afternoon until two thirty. Buku hot. Had off at night and had beer and burgers at *Bundy's Hootch*.

May 15

Had to go on bunkers in morning. Had afternoon off. Had to go on bunkers at night with Howe. Quite drowsy.

May 16

Had most of day off to prepare for movement to "C" company area. Supposed to go to OP-5 but beat it. Listened to records at night.

May 17

Moved to "C" company area. Few blocks from the beach. Flat area. Mostly pine trees. Have nice bunker. Pulled bunkers at night. Moon out, bright.

May 18

Had morning off, so read a book. Had patrol in afternoon about three thousand meters. Tough to walk in sand, stayed in bunker at night.

Author with Combat Gear

May 19

Had day off, so slept some during day. Had ambush at night. Air base supposed to be mortared tonight but nothing.

May 20

Had day off, so tried to sleep a little. Finished the book *Manchurian Candidate*. Took shower in Rauvala's well-shower. No. 1. Pulled bunkers in #3 at night.

May 21

Went on about four-thousand-meter patrol today. Went swimming in afternoon at beach. Water warm and refreshing. Pulled bunkers at night as usual.

May 22

Had morning and afternoon off. Had 7,400-meter ambush patrol, squad size. Longest patrol ever at night. Captain psycho chased by water buffalo on way back. Buku tired.

May 23

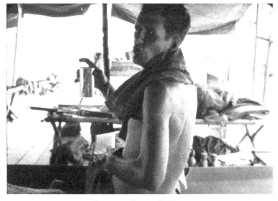

Doc in Squad Tent

Had nothing to do all day, so just listened to Doc's radio. Captain caught Doc and me at fence, talking to

Vietnamese. No sweat though. Gunships fired on estimated VC about seven thousand meters away.

Doc Clowning Around

May 24

Had patrol in afternoon, buku hot. On standby for second squad out on ambush. They spotted buku VC. Fired on them but no bodies left. Not much sleep tonight.

May 25

Had most of day off, so just rested. "C" company came in today, had ambush tonight about 1,200 meters. Moon out. Bright but quiet.

Monahan by Bunker

May 26

Went back into base camp today. Had to cut grass around the tent in afternoon. Had night off for once. Slept pretty good.

May 27

Had to clean up hooch. General came today to inspect. Had afternoon and night off. Saw *Man From U.N.C.L.E.* movie. Repeat. Sweet dreams.

May 28

Company went on three-day operation, but I stayed back. Time for a break. Pulled some details during day. Had night off and watched movie *Torn Curtain*. Real good.

May 29

Rode shotgun for Savedo most of the day, so didn't pull any details. No movie tonight so listened to music on radio. Slept good.

May 30

Rode shotgun for Savedo today again. Brought *McCray* back from brigade. Had garbage detail in afternoon had CQ at night. Not too bad though.

May 31

Had off today because of CQ night before, not really. Had *IG* inspection and got paid. Had to go on bunkers at night. Listened to good music.

June

—

June 1

Helped build ammo bunker today. Had to go on bunkers in late afternoon but had night off. Saw movie *The Las Vegas Hillbillys*. Pretty good.

June 2

Had to lower tent in morning. Had afternoon off. Ambush tonight but no more ambushes or S-and-D for me. Buku, happy. Saw movie *McGuire, Go Home!* Pretty good. Buku rain tonight.

Cow with Hat

June 3

Beat work in morning. Bought a radio at brigade, *Sony*. Went on OP-7 at night had about eleven guys. Buku sleep. Quiet as usual.

June 4

Had morning off but had to work on squad bunker in afternoon. Change 101. Had bunkers at night. Bunker 10 on top.

June 5

Troops at Bunker

Had morning off but not really. Harassment and worked on squad bunker in afternoon. Had night off, so had small party. Slept like a rock.

June 6

Had to work all day in bunker. Put new top on it. Different change every day. Had OP-6 at night. Didn't sleep much but quiet.

June 7

Rice Paddies

Had morning off, so just rested. Had to go on bunkers in afternoon and read books. Had night off. So went to watch movie, *Marriage Italian Style*. Pretty good.

June 8

Had bunkers in morning until noon. Went down brigade PX in afternoon also filled some sandbags back here. Had bunkers at night with Howe. Tee-tee sleep.

June 9

Had morning off and just goofed off. Worked a little on filling sandbags in afternoon. Had night off, so drank some beer and slept like a rock.

June 10

Author with Troops Building Bunker

Had mine sweep this morning. Worked a little in afternoon. Had bunker 4 at night. Rained and miserable. Nine had some incoming rifle grenades.

June 11

Had day off because of ambush tonight. Thought I was through with ambushes, but guess I was mistaken. Five men to a position, plenty of sleep.

June 12

Had morning off but had detail in afternoon; off at night, so had big beer party. Pretty good time, but ended at 9:10 p.m. when Looey broke it up.

June 13

Had day off to prepare for one-day operation tomorrow. No beer for sale. Good movie with Elke Sommer. Have to wake up at 4:00 a.m.

June 14

Got up at four o'clock for walking company operations near village. Searched huts. Came back in afternoon. Got drunk at night and saw *The Outrage*. Blantz.

June 15

Had to go out in rice paddies to secure LZ for chopper. Eagle Flight for convoy but no trouble, so no sweat. Had 2,200-meter platoon ambush at night. Quiet.

June 16

Had morning off because of ambush before. Went to PX in afternoon and bought buku goodies. Had night off except for night ride to OP-6 *and stand to.*

June 17

Had to go out to OP-5 in the morning. Came back in afternoon and just rested. Platoon drank buku beer in afternoon. Had bunkers at night.

June 18

Had morning off, so slept for a few hours. Went to brigade for money order in afternoon. Had night off. "A" company had two guys wounded when they sprung ambush.

June 19

Goofed off in morning. Had to dig sump for shower in afternoon. Buku hot today, about 120 degrees. Had OP-6 at night. "A" company ambush stayed at OP, getting too short.

June 20

Had road sweep in morning. Got drunk in early afternoon and slept until five fifteen. Had to go on OP-5 at night. *Moon out bright. Windy stayed awhile.*

June 21

Stayed out on OP-5 during morning and had afternoon off. Replacements due tomorrow. Hip, hip, *hooray*. Had night off but no movie. Too bad.

June 22

Had morning off except for hassle inspection. Worked a little in afternoon, sandbagging. Had night off because of airmobile operation tomorrow. Too short.

June 23

Went out on airmobile operation to look for *missile sites*. Hassle. Hot LZ, but didn't know about it. Buku weight on back. Unbelievable ambush got there at 10:00 p.m.

June 24

Today we swept some more *missile sites*. Trucked back at 2:00 p.m. Buku tired. Saw "*Signpost to Danger*, Alfred Hitchcock thriller, then slept, *zzzz*.

June 25

Worked a little in morning and hid in afternoon. Copped small high. Saw movie *Your Cheatin' Heart*, Sharp's favorite. Sweet dreams.

June 26

Went out to "B" company while they went out on operation. Visited Tony in kitchen and got some chow. Had night off. Too hot to sleep much.

June 27

Had road sweep in morning and S-and-D at ten o'clock. Hot walking. Got back at 3:00 p.m. in time for bunkers. Pretty busy day.

June 28

Had off during the day, so read a book. Hot in hooch, but cool in bunker. Had ambush tonight. Ridiculous. Left after dark. Didn't sleep much.

June 29

Had day off because of ambush night before. Read a book and slept a little. Had night off, so saw Tony in mess hall. Baked a small cake for me.

June 30

Had short patrol in morning, squad size. Read book in afternoon. Had bunkers at night. Have new platoon leader, Petrin. Had basic with.

July

—

July 1

Had day off, but some of platoon went out on S-and-D, three wounded from second squad, tripped booby trap. Had ambush tonight. Got about two hours sleep.

July 2

Had day off, so read books and stayed in bunker. Got port call for July 7, numbah 1. Had night off.

July 3

Had day off again. Platoon went out, but *old-timers* stayed back. About time we got a break. Saw movie at night, *Horror Castle*. Gory. Pleasant dreams.

July 4

Came back in from "B" company today. Got small high at NCO club on bunkers but argued out of it. Pleasant dreams.

July 5

Movie Screen in Base Camp

Had nothing to do, so went to brigade in morning and bought suitcase. Went into town in afternoon and bought souvenirs. Had night off; saw movie *Wild Seed*.

July 6

Started processing through battalion. Stopped at NCO club and copped high. Saw English movie at night. Didn't sleep much.

July 7

Went down brigade for final processing. Buku lines. Got out about 5:00 p.m. Rained at night plus idiot alert. Last night in company. Good riddance.

July 8

Went to airport and got ride to Tan Son Nhut. By bus to Long Binh, *past MACV*. Got bunk and drunk at club. Buku harassment by NCOs.

July 9

Most of 3/21 out on two flights. Just have to wait. Went to club with *Black Sheep* and raised hell. Took name tags off. No identity. Sweet dreams.

July 10

Author at Long Binh

Supposed to fly back at 8:30 p.m., but flight canceled for eleven hours. Beat details, not much longer to go.

July 11

Finally got flight out at five thirty. Stopped at Yokota, Japan; Anchorage, Alaska; and McGuire Air Force Base, New Jersey. Back to civilization.

July 12

Wen to Fort Dix and started processing. Had physical and got summer greens. Went to NCO club at night, buku beer.

July 13

Processed until about four-thirty afternoon. Went home with Dennis and mother. Happy acquaintances. Glad to be back. Numbah 1.

Departing Anchorage, Alaska

Last Leg to McGuire AFB over Canadian Rockies

What Was Your Favorite Memory of Your Time in Vietnam?

We were on a Forward Helo Base of the 1ˢᵗ Infantry Division, the "Big Red One," after Operation Attleboro in November '66. We were on a daytime patrol. Well, the platoon was *taking a break*, and the sergeant decided to have me and another trooper *take a break* in the middle of a field with the sun blaring down. The rest of the platoon was in the shade of the jungle, and I could never figure out why. Well, along a trail nearby came a farmer who I will call "Papasan" with his oxcart. He stopped and saw us there and came over to us and proceeded to build us a "lean-to" from bamboo stakes and a thatched roof to shade us from the sun. At that moment, I thought of the sheer humanity of the farmer to attempt to help us. I wanted to reward the farmer. We did not speak the same language. The only item I had to give Papasan was a folding knife I had purchased, and I gave it to him.

This is a moment that will stay with me forever.

November 10, 1966

Denny,

Hi, buddy. This is going to be an unusual letter because I won't answer all of your questions. The reason being we just got back from a six-day mission, and we go out on a patrol tomorrow. You read about the mortar attack on the base. We had a fourteen-man ambush patrol 1,300 meters from the spot the VC fired their mortars from. We just sat there and waited for them to come our way, but they never did. I was shaking like a leaf. They had something like six 82 mm soviet mortars, approximately seventy-two men with automatic weapons. We wouldn't be here today if we went to get them that night. We had two killed and fifty-seven wounded; we didn't get any of them!

We just came back from six days at Boi Loi Woods; you probably read about it in the papers. A regiment of VC was there. We didn't see much action, but we got two wounded in the platoon. The second battalion, twenty-seventh infantry, lost twenty-seven guys out of a company. We saw the dead; what a pitiful sight. The "Big Red One" moved in and took over, resulting over eight hundred VC killed plus countless equipment found. Our first big operation, we came out "Smelling like a rose" again. We have another operation soon. So if you don't get mail from me right away, you will know that I am on the operation.

That guy, Tony Scivolini, who had the piece in the paper is the "Perpetual Smiler" who had to stay in the "Leaning Rest" position at Newark; I'm surprised that you didn't remember the name; I gave him the article, and he was surprised. The cook's job is taken in the company; I would feel guilty if I stayed back while my buddies went out on missions. Tony probably didn't tell you, but he paid for the job about $100. I'd have a guilty conscience if I did that; I hope you understand; I'm enclosing a money order for $ 8 for *Playboy*, soothe.

Well, I guess I'll close for now; my next letter will be more organized. Say hello to me to everyone and write soon.

Your pal,
Dave Guard

PS: I don't mind telling you, I love the Kingston Trio.

The Unwritten Rule to Take Care of Each Other and Stick Together

Hi Nora,

The following is a recap of the story I told you yesterday of an incident that occurred during my tour of duty in Vietnam.

On occasions, we would be assigned to assist in guarding a bridge on Highway 1 overnight with South Vietnam Marines so that the enemy would not "Blow up the Bridge" and halt traffic on this busy *dirt highway*.

I have attached a picture taken probably that day with some troops and a Viet Marine. At the extreme left of the picture, I am holding an M2 carbine rifle.

Author with Monahan with M-2 Carbine

This was the best highway in Vietnam.

On this particular night, we have eight troops with us, which was good as we only had to have one troop on guard each hour.

I was on guard approximately 2:00 a.m., walking near the middle of the bridge, when suddenly, there occurred a "Fire Fight" south of our position approximately one kilometer down the road. My thought was that a US Marine Tiger Team was in trouble as I observed red tracers," which I knew we used, and also green tracers, which I knew the enemy used. Anyway, the incident was not endangering our position. So I just observed the firefight for a few minutes and returned to our bunker where all the troops were *copping Zs* soundly sleeping, when I heard our PRC-25 pack radio blaring from battalion that they thought we were under attack and were saddling up troops to come down to rescue us. Since I was the only troop awake, I assured them that we were not under attack, and the "Sitrep was negative." The rest of the night was quiet. When they sent down trucks in the AM to bring us back to our base camp, they asked who was on *watch* during the incident. We did not tell them. If we did, I probably would have gotten an *Article 15* for insubordination. A prime example of our unwritten rule is to "take care of each other and stick together."

So what da ya think?

Your war correspondent,
Jim

Call sign: Romeo 11

CPSIA information can be obtained
at www.ICGtesting.com
Printed in the USA
BVHW021015111122
651752BV00018B/323